CONTENTS

Foreword	06
History Of The Liver Birds	08
Meet The Birdman	12
The Beginning	14
1910-2000s	16
Here And Now	36
Liver Birds On TV	38
Frank Carlyle, Me And My Bird	40
Birdspotting	42
The Echo and the Liver Bird	52
Fly Past For The Birds	54
Feathered Fact File	60
Timeless	62
What Do The Birds Do?	64
Beaking From The Heart	66
And These Birds Can Sing	78
Upwards And Onwards	82

Trinity Mirror Media

Compiled by Peter Grant
Sub Editing: Vicky Andrews, James Cleary, Michael McGuinness
Design: Zoe Bevan

Pictures courtesy of Liverpool Daily Post & Echo Archive.
With special thanks to Robin Bird for the use of the Bob Bird and Keith Medley photographs

ISBN 9781906802837

To buy prints of the images in this publication, or any photos in our fantastic archive collection, log on to www.merseyshop.com/buyaphoto or telephone 0845 300 3021

FINE FEATHERED FRIENDS

FOREWORD, by Peter Grant

WATCHING and waiting, some people say they are like protective parents, constant in this ever-changing, great city.

We look up to them – literally and emotionally – in times of celebration and sorrow. They are our re-assurance.

Bombs have fallen, riots have raged, commerce can suffer. But they stand resolute. Their expressions won't alter, but you can't help believing they laugh and dream, rage and weep with us.

They have seen everything. They have witnessed some world-changing events, looked on proudly at all the Liverpool firsts that have occurred in their 100 years as Guardians. They are chronicled here in this special centenary souvenir publication, a real bird's eye view of a century.

If the Liver Birds ever fly away, the city will fall into the sea, so says the legend...maybe it's best to keep them tied down.

In this glossy birthday card with a difference you will see them arrive in 1911, and stand atop the Liver Building in 2011.

They never age – one gazing out to sea looking after the sailors, ships and travellers, who keep an eye on Birkenhead.

The other looks over the city, to see when the pubs open...

A lighthouse with a difference – the Liver Building – often wrongly (but affectionately) called 'The Liver Buildings' is as welcoming as the Statue of Liberty in New York

"They have witnessed some world-changing events, looked proudly on at all the Liverpool firsts that have occurred in their 100 years as Guardians"

The Liver Birds mean something different to everyone. They are unique – no other city has a symbol like it.

They are old friends – we are all old friends.

In this biography of their Liverpool lives – 100 years not out – they are as alive and vibrant as ever.

And they are not camera shy, as our Post and Echo archive reveals.

Celebrities say why they mean so much to them, too.

So, dear Liver Birds, here's to the next 100 years.

Soar on...

On a wing and a prayer: A clean-up exercise supervised by a health and safety man without vertigo (he didn't have far to go – he lived around the corner)

THE SPIRIT OF LIVERPOOL

The magic and the mystery of the legendary Liver Bird

WHERE in the world is there a symbol which is so immediately identifiable with the city it represents? Mention the Liver Bird in any far-flung corner of the globe and people will instantly know you are referring to Liverpool.

In the city itself the Liver Bird is portrayed, often with great imagination, as livery and logo for companies and clubs, council and colleges, public houses and public parks, launderettes and litter bins. The Liver Bird is on the logo of the city council, Liverpool University, John Moores University and, of course, Liverpool Football Club.

Perhaps the greatest manifestation of its universality was the attempt by Liverpool FC to trademark their version of the bird in 2008, in an effort to halt rampant false merchandising. It was a move that received short shrift, with the then deputy council leader, Flo Clucas, commenting: "The Liver Bird belongs to all the people of Liverpool and not one company or organisation."

What other city has such a celebrity creature at its helm, and why is this universally recognisable representation of the city, its people, its history, its culture and tradition, shrouded in mystery?

WHAT IS THE LIVER BIRD?

IN 2011 the 18ft tall copper giants atop the Liver Building on Liverpool's impressive waterfront celebrate their 100th birthday. These two creations are not only the most famous of the famous, but they clearly show the confusion that exists in that they are neither eagle nor cormorant, or any other known species.

Some say cormorant, dove or spoonbill, others think eagle – while many believe it is a purely mythical creation. William Enfield, a Liverpool historian writing in 1774, maintained that it existed only in 'fabulous tradition', meaning it was a creature of invention like the Phoenix. Looking around the city the confusion is manifest, with the bird existing in so many different shapes and sizes. Almost anything with a leaf in its beak passes for a Liver Bird.

Why has the Liver Bird, which is so linked to the origins and history of the city, become such a confused symbol? It is indeed a creature of much myth, mistake, misinterpretation and maltreatment, often by those charged with its custodianship.

History, it seems, has not been kind to the memory of the most famous bird in the world. ➤

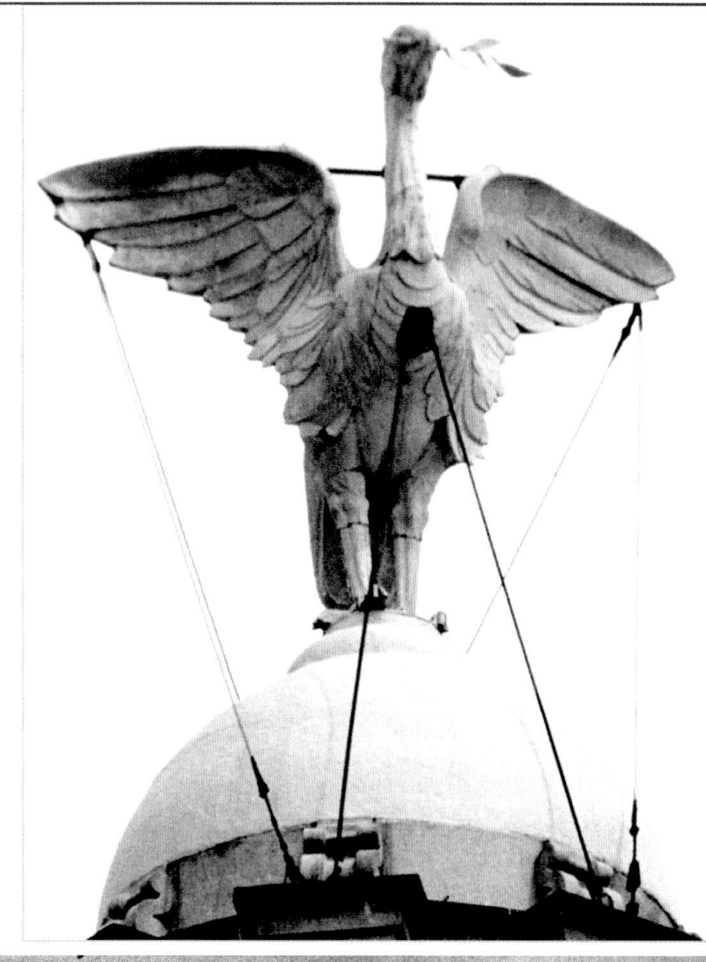

Alfred Hitchcock could have been inspired to make his classic film *The Birds* by this eerie scene taken by an amateur photographer in 1931, a shot of gulls around the Liver Building

Images of King John and seal, courtesy of Liverpool records office

LOCATION, LOCATION, LOCATION

TO trace the origins of the Liver Bird we have to start with the long and, for many centuries, uneventful history of Liverpool itself.

It is believed the first tiny settlement, scrapping sustenance from sea and soil, can be dated as far back as the 1st century AD. For hundreds of years it remained obscure and unimportant, always in the shadow of its close neighbour, the bustling port of Chester, and was even unworthy of a mention in the Domesday Book in 1086. However, in 1207, the unpopular and much maligned King John needed a port to serve as a point of dispatch for troops to Ireland. Unwilling to enlist the support of the Earl of Chester, one of his many enemies, he granted a Royal Charter to Liverpool, essentially an invitation 'letters of patent' to people to take up holdings, small pieces of land known as burgages. These areas were available at very attractive prices, initially one shilling (5p) per year, while Liverpool also became exempt from certain taxes. It was a small start, but laid the foundations for the settlement to grow and attract trade.

KING JOHN 1167–1216

"JOHN was a tyrant. He was a wicked ruler who did not behave like a king. He was greedy and took as much money as he could from his people. Hell is too good for a horrible person like him."

– Matthew Paris, 13th century chronicler.

It is perhaps a shame that the monarch who gave the city its charter is one of the least popular, and least respected, kings in history. In 2006 he was chosen by *BBC History Magazine* as the 13th century's worst Briton. During his life he acquired two nicknames: "Lackland", as the youngest of five sons he inherited no estates from his father, Henry II. Moreover, whilst king, he lost territory to France and thus the monikor "Softsword", due to his perceived lack of prowess in battle. Ill-tempered, lecherous father of many illegitimate children, arch enemy of popular legend Robin Hood, attempted usurper of his brother's throne, excommunicated by the Pope, kicked out of Ireland after only a few months of his leadership and cowed into sealing the Magna Carta, conceding power to his barons.

He even managed to lose the Crown Jewels in a bog in East Anglia!

His older brother, Richard I, was a much more exciting and romantic figure. Richard, the crusading 'Lionheart' of a king, was the founding father of Portsmouth and history has been much kinder to his memory. In truth, medieval kings all tended to be ruthless and cruel individuals, and John did have his good points. Moreover, like many before and after him, he was beset by enemies at every turn.

John was responsible for the building of the historic London Bridge. He was an effective administrator, had considerable ability as a strategic thinker and is credited with the creation of the modern Royal Navy. He built royal

"When the long tally is added, it will be seen that the British nation and the English-speaking world owe far more to the vices of John than to the labours of virtuous sovereigns" – Winston Churchill

harbours, installed an Admiralty, oversaw major improvements in ship design and commissioned the first big transport ships.

For all his faults, he will be remembered fondly in Merseyside as the king who created Liverpool.

In 1229, Henry III granted Liverpool a second charter, which enabled the use of a common seal. This seal became the first indication that the city honoured its founder by adopting the eagle as the official symbol of the city.

This seal depicts a crudely carved bird, more eagle than anything else and, under the breast the words JOHIS or IOH'IS are engraved. This is an abbreviation for the Latin 'Johannis' or John. It could refer to King John, St John or both, for the eagle was the ancient symbol of St John, whom King John acknowledged as his patron saint.

ANCIENT SEAL OF LIVERPOOL

Moreover, a sun and a crescent moon are also carved near the bird's beak, symbols used on John's Irish coinage. In the bird's beak is a sprig of foliage, almost certainly broom or 'planta genista', which is another symbol of the royal house of the Plantagenets. It was originally spelt 'Plante Genest', 'Plantegenest' or 'Plantaginet', from which the name is derived and originated with Geoffrey of Anjou, father of King Henry II of England and grandfather of King John's. It is believed that Geoffrey of Anjou wore a sprig of it in his bonnet or he planted it to improve his covered hides for hunting. There's even a theory that he used a bunch of broom twigs to beat or scourge himself, as was the religious practice of the time.

It was thought to be an important plant because of its golden flower and because people believed it to have a spiritual power.

This is very strong evidence that the Liver Bird is indeed the eagle, making the seal itself a hugely important historical and cultural artefact to the city.

The earliest surviving example of this seal is an impression dating from 1352. Unfortunately, this vital piece of heritage is nowhere to be seen; not in the Town Hall, nor in one of the city's magnificent museums or anywhere else in Liverpool. Or is it?

An illusion: The demolition of the Dock estate at the South End of the Princess Dock exposed a tree which made it look as if the Liver Bird had perched elsewhere

Rick Myers displaying some of his popular Liver Bird designs

MEET THE BIRDMAN

A bird or two in the hand means a lot to sculptor Rick Myers – he has studied and created versions of the Liver Birds for 20 years

RICK'S works, in all shapes and sizes, have flown to more than 40 countries around the world, and been presented to dignitaries visiting Liverpool.

A well-respected charity fundraiser, Rick has a passion for the birds and has just finished writing and illustrating a children's book about their history.

He has also created his latest, modern incarnation of the bird, 'The Spirit of Liverpool', to mark the centenary of the opening of the Royal Liver Building.

Rick's versions of the bird became popular as awards for numerous events in the region, in particular for the annual BBC Scouseology awards, when statuettes were presented to celebrities linked to the area, as well as the Merseyside Tourism awards.

The bird was used by Liverpool City Council as gifts for visiting VIPs, and hundreds were sold to Scousers at home and abroad, being particularly popular with Liverpool FC fans.

They are also the trophies for two poets in 2011, who will partake in the Pause for Hope Cancer Performance at Liverpool Anglican Cathedral.

Says modest Rick: "'Ex-pats seemed to love them, and they are now 'nesting' all over the globe."

Explaining why he felt a new image should be added to his vast 'Liver Bird Family', he smiles.

"I have the greatest respect for the work of Carl Bartels, who created the birds that sit on top of the Liver Building.

"They reflect their time perfectly as Liverpool was entering the 20th century and the magnificent Liver Building had been completed.

"I suspect they will always remain the Liver Birds in the eyes of most Liverpudlians.

"But I felt it was also time for a new, modern, dynamic bird that reflects the new Liverpool, which we see around us now without losing the original spirit.

"The Spirit of Liverpool can sit happily alongside the Liver Building birds in the 21st century."

Liver Birds Inc Ltd says it all – set up by its feathered friends to market the Spirit of Liverpool models.

Directors Rick, Paul Andrew, MD of Punchline Media and Events Ltd and Arthur Johnson, a former senior journalist with the Liverpool Daily Post & Echo, are all life-long fans of the bird, and all it means.

Some of the Echo's SOB campaigners including sports editor Ken Rogers (second left) and editor John Griffith (centre)

Arthur recalls: "When I was features editor of the Echo some years ago there was a suggestion that the Liver Birds should be removed from the city council logo.

"This sparked public outrage and we launched a campaign SOB (Save Our Bird). Thousands of people around the world signed our petition, and the bird was saved.

"This just shows how much the image means. There is a great affection for it. But it has developed over the centuries and I believe Rick's new Spirit of Liverpool is just right for the city today."

Paul Andrew agrees: "This new iconic version is beautiful and, for me, represents all that is good about the city, its people and our famous spirit."

Rick is honoured that his Liver Bird influence has captured the imagination: "I am thrilled the Liver Bird models are on someone's shelf somewhere around the world. I am proud, as proud as the two birds who symbolise Liverpool across the globe."

For further details of The Spirit of Liverpool Birds go to ***www.liverbirdsinc.com***

WE ARE ON OUR WAY

It is 1910 and the Liver Birds have yet to be hatched atop the Chicago-styled skyscraper. The moment the two Scouse superstars arrive they make an instant global impact.

A BIRD'S EYE VIEW

Laughter and Tears

The Liver Birds have seen it all.
The Liver Birds have heard it all.
First World War
Second World War
Recession
Football Triumphs
Football Disasters
Downturn in fortunes in the 80s
Upturn in fortunes with European Capital of Culture
They had a bird's eye view of history in the making.
Here are some moments from the decades where, perched on top, they saw the changing face of the city and the world.
They have travelled all over the globe – those two Liver Birds – but they never left once. Magical.

LIVER TIMELINE

- ***1899*** – Oliver Lodge invents the car ignition system.
- ***1901*** – Liverpool runs the first anti-tubercolosis campaign in Britain.
- ***1902*** – The School of Tropical Medicine is the first medical institution to gain the Nobel Prize for Medicine for connecting the mosquito with malaria.
- ***1904*** – The University of Liverpool founds the first school of veterinary science in the country.
- ***1907*** – The Liver Building has the world's largest clock faces, the first large-scale ferro concrete building in the world and Europe's first skyscraper.
- ***1908*** – Birkenhead founds the first ever Boy Scouts Group.
- ***1909*** – Eleanor Rathbone becomes the first woman councillor and Woolworths opens its first British store in Church Street.

The Birds become the official ambassadors of the city. You can leave, start a new life or set up in another city, but these birds will always be here

"In the first year that the Liver Birds first roost on top of the buiding the city stops with the start of the General Transport Strike"

LIVER TIMELINE

- ***1911*** – In the first year that the Liver Birds first roost on top of the building the city stops with the start of the General Transport Strike. First they see the seamen walk out, followed by a great demonstration and march by the Transport Workers' Federation. It escalated into a general transport strike involving 70,000 people, including railway workers.

- ***1912*** – Across from the feet of the city facing the Liver Birds, crowds wait outside the offices of the White Star Line in James Street for news of the Titanic.

- ***1913*** – Looking over the rooftops, the Meccano factory is seen to open in Binns Road.

- ***1914*** – Our brave soldiers march off to war. The Birds wave them off with sadness.

- ***1915*** – Once again the eyes that watch the sea fill with tears, as the Lusitania sinks on her way to Liverpool.

The roaring twenties: The First World War is over and Liverpool is getting back on its webbed feet. Already the waterfront appeal of the Birds and the building is attracting attention from tourists

LIVER TIMELINE

- **1920** – The Birds see the first all welded hulled ship, Fullagar, built at Laird's Shipyard.

- **1923** – Littlewoods Pools open their world famous organisation.

- **1925** – The Liverpool Empire opens, as does the first Juvenile Court, in Crosshall Street. The Birds blink as lights are switched on and electricity supplies the city for the first time.

- **1928** – Dixie Dean scores his 60th league goal for Everton in the 1927/28 season. The Spion Kop is rebuilt, becoming the League's largest covered terrace. A survey shows that Liverpool has one of the highest rates of poverty in the country.

LIVER TIMELINE

- ***1932*** – The gloves are on as the first purpose-built boxing stadium in Britain opens in Bixteth Street.
- ***1933*** – The sky's the limit as Speke Airport opens.
- ***1934*** – Progress marches on as the Queensway tunnel is opened by King George V, while New Brighton Open Air Pool is also established.
- ***1939*** – The Thetis submarine sinks. More dark days ahead as a world war is declared again.

Reflections at the Salthouse Dock: It's 1933 and there are storm clouds gathering over Europe as the Liver Birds look on

DISTRICT BANK
CASTLE STREET
ENT
AIR RAID SHELTER

Above: In 1949 the Liver Birds look down as work goes on at the restoration of the George's Landing stage. Famous Merseyside photographers Medley and Bird (not Liver Bird) of Wallasey saw work going on at the base of one of the bridges. And, judging by the clock, it was just in time for a tea break

Liver Bird salute on August 8 1940. A home defence battalion marches past Liverpool Town Hall. The upstairs salute was taken by the two Liver Birds wishing our brave troops love and luck as they marched off to war. Down below, the salute was taken by Lord Mayor Sir Sidney Jones and Brigadier T.T. Waddington

LIVER TIMELINE

- ***1940*** – During the Blitz, on 29th November, a shelter in the basement of Earnest Brown Junior Instructional Centre suffers a direct hit with the loss of 166 men, women and children. This was the worst loss of life in a single incident.

- ***1941*** – The Birds keep mum in the Battle of the Atlantic as the Western Approaches Command Centre operates from secret headquarters under Derby House.

- ***1947*** – Liverpool win first post-war league championship.

Those Liver Birds get everywhere: Here a clever shot from 1957 shows the Celestial Globe at the Pier Head – the Seaman's memorial depicting the ancient signs of the Zodiac – designed by sculptor Mr H Tyson Smith

The Birds tower above 'one more unlovely adornment of the Pier Head' (as captioned by the Echo), a former fire station, used as a clubroom for pensioners in August 1957

LIVER TIMELINE

- ***1952*** – The Birds wave off the first package holiday flight leaving from Speke Airport.

- ***1953*** – They cheer for our glorious Queen Elizabeth II at her Coronation.

- ***1956*** – Goodbye to the end of the Dockers Umbrella – the overhead railway.

- ***1957*** – They have got the beat in their beaks as The Cavern opens in Mathew Street. They know something 'special' is going to happen in that cellar full of noise.

A Liver Bird in captivity: Liverpool Town Hall's original Liver Bird is encased forever in 1961. His batman is Ernest Phillips, butler to the Lord Mayor. (Below right) In the University of Liverpool's campus you can find the Liver Bird on flower pots (Honorary Degree)

"The Birds notice a young band called The Beatles leaving for Hamburg"

The Liver Bird in close-up: One of the early Paparazzi shots of the bird – tied down by copper wire – but happy to stay put, 1965

LIVER TIMELINE

- ***1960*** – The Birds notice a young band called The Beatles leaving for Hamburg.
- ***1962*** – Technology takes over as Mersey Docks and Harbour company become the first port in Britain to use a computer.
- ***1964*** – A solemn moment as the last execution in Britain is carried out at Walton Prison.
- ***1967*** – They pay respects as the Metropolitan Cathedral of Christ the King is consecrated.

By Royal Appointment: Her Majesty in 1977 celebrates her Jubilee, while the Birds look at Prince Phillip and say: "Who is one looking at?"

Above: Meet Dorothy and Enid, two oldish Liver birds. The Liver Birds and the building below it have often been immortalised in print, books...and as a cake. Four hundred and four separate pieces were made by these two students at Liverpool Colquitt Technical College in 1979. The cake raised money for Alder Hey Hospital

It's clean up time: The world famous photographer Bob Bird of the Picture People dynasty took this photo of the 'other' birds having a makeover, 1973

LIVER TIMELINE

- ***1970*** – The Birds share their sky view as Liverpool Museum opens Britain's first public planetarium.

- ***1971*** – There should always be two of everything. The second Mersey Tunnel, Kingsway, is opened by Princess Anne.

- ***1978*** – Another call for respect as the Anglican Cathedral is finally completed 68 years after the foundation stone was laid.

Bird bath – Time for the five-year clean up: Walter Hewitt and Sons of Warrington had a tall order. And there he was, scaling new heights to make sure the building clock face and birds looked good

Keeping it in the family – Steeplejack Bob Hewitt is giving the birds a tidy up in 1995

LIVER TIMELINE

- ***1993*** – The Birds brace for the hardest of truths as the two-year-old James Bulger is murdered by two 10-year-old boys.

- ***1994*** – The Birds remember Roy Vivian Hughes MBE, the civil engineer for Merseyrail underground, as his ashes are interred in an underground concourse wall in Moorfields station – the first person to be legally buried in a railway station.

- ***1995*** – The docks are restless once more as the Liverpool Dock Strikes begin. The dispute runs for three years.

- ***1996*** – A musical progress as the birds brush up on their beats when LIPA opens.

The biggest stage ever constructed in Europe for the John Lennon tribute show at the Pier Head, 1990. Yoko Ono and a galaxy of stars performed, while the Liver Birds allegedly danced

LIVER TIMELINE

- ***2006*** – The Pier Head landing stage sinks as the tide rushes in after an unusually low water.
- ***2007*** – It's been a long time coming: the newly opened cruise liner terminal welcomes it's first vessel – the Seven Seas Voyager.
- ***2008*** – Liverpool's Capital of Culture year see the eyes of the world on the city again, with events including the Clipper Round The World Yacht Race (pictured). The Liverpool ECHO Arena opens on the city's waterfront.

SUNSET OVER THE CITY

Parr Street co-owner, politician, music producer and photographer Gary Millar is a neighbour of the Liver Birds. His images and thoughts reflect the ever-changing city he has grown to love, along with those ever changing birds

GARY believes that bands and artists like Coldplay and Barry Manilow, who have recorded in the city, loved it, too.

He said: "Every day I see the Liver Birds. Every day I walk through the city and they just pop out of the blue as if to surprise you. In my city centre apartment I look at them through the window.

"I often think of the people over the past century who have passed through this great city and I think about just what these two birds have seen.

"They have seen it all – ups and downs – and yet we feel reassured they will be there, no matter what is happening. I am from Edinburgh – but this is my adopted city. I have been to a wedding underneath the Liver Birds – or should that be 'Lover Birds'?

"Each new sunset is a brand new day, a new hope and a new horizon. The birds may be 100 years old, but like all Liverpudlians they are thinking of the next 100 years, starting now.

"They are keeping their wings crossed that things are on the up, and they will be – as long as those two centurions are there. A new dawn – a new sunset. That's the Liver Birds for me and I hope, you."

LIGHTS, CAMERA, ACTION!

Colin McKeown is passionate about filming in his home town. So when he produced the ratings winning police drama Liverpool One, he knew he wanted his TWO lucky charms in there

THE multi-award winning film director has worked with the biggest names in showbiz, but none he says are as BIG as the Liver Birds (and he didn't have to pay them).

The BAFTA for best supporting stars are...The Liver Birds. Colin says: "Liverpool One is a show, which will always have emotional resonance with myself because it has afforded me the opportunity to show my city at its best.

"What has become clear to me over the years is that Liverpool is a beautiful city, but it's even more beautiful in the night time and strangely, the form and shape of the place with its iconic buildings changes, given how it is illuminated.

"For instance...as day gives way to twilight the sun cascades across the Mersey and creates a sort of lateral golden light. Most film-makers dub this 'Liverpool's Golden Hour' and, depending on the season, it is about 4-5pm. It evokes a quality of light that is saught after universally. That light fades... Liverpool emerges from its own illumination as the night sets in.

"Nothing is more synonymous with Liverpool than the Liver Birds. One looking out; one looking in and both of them covering each other's back, demonstrating a sort of authorial loyalty that is intrinsic to Liverpool.

"Film making is about capturing the moment although often producing and manufacturing that moment can be at odds with reality. In one scene where I had to capture the Liver Building, embodied by the Liver Birds, we had to mechanically turn back time and wind the clock face back so it fitted the narrative of the scene. Whether the Liver Birds were actually happy about being unwitting time travellers I'll never know! But that night, what was called for pictorially was the Liver Birds to be at their photographic best. We needed to bring them

Elizabeth Estensen and Nerys Hughes, two of 'the Birds' in Carla Lane's hit sitcom

out from the building, magnify their majestic image and what they demanded was extra attention, more focused light to be directed on them.

"So, that night, there they stood like two temperamental divas demanding more care and attention from the film-making crew for their close- ups.

"The whole scene took more than two hours longer than we had originally scheduled, not for any reasons of ego or mood swings from a troublesome artiste, but simply because to get the correct image the Liver Birds deserved extra care and resources were warranted.

"Eventually the lighting was right, the frame was set and I couldn't be certain, but just before the cameras were about to roll I am sure I could hear the satisfied announcement from both of these cormorants, which seemed to say: "Ready when you are, Mr DeMille."

STAR OF THE SHOW

The most famous portrayal of the Liver Birds came courtesy of Carla Lane, a TV series in the 70s not of our sculpted friends but two Dolly Birds. The sitcom showed the city in a good light the minute the credits rolled and the cameras panned around the waterfront.

The Liver Birds ran from 1969 to 1978, and re-emerged for a revival in 1996. In the pilot and first series Sandra and Beryl were played first by Polly James and Pauline Collins. Later Nerys Hughes and Elizabeth Estensen became the fab, funny flat-sharing females. Polly and Nerys were reunited in the mid-90s, but it didn't enjoy the same success – although 10 series was an incredible achievement.

On stage, the Liver Birds have appeared all over the world from Liverpool to the USA and Japan thanks to the brilliant backdrop to Willy Russell's *Blood Brothers*. The Liver Building and the two birds make a stark supporting 'star' in this world famous musical. And whenever a film crew arrives in the city the Liver Birds make guest appearances, including in 1985 British comedy *Letter to Brezhnev*.

ME AND MY BIRD

Public speaker, BBC broadcaster, historian and columnist Frank Carlyle talks about a lifelong love affair

WHEN people mention the Liver Bird, it might sound silly, but it reminds me of me!

Yes, I'm the 'Liver Bird', just like every other Scouser.

So what does the 'Bird' represent to our city and its people and, most importantly, what does it mean to myself?

Once King John's 1207 Royal Charter document was stamped with the Eagle of St John, it has become synonymous with the identity of our city and its citizens.

The 'Eagle' or as we affectionately know it, the Liver Bird, has become a big family crest to all Liverpudlians.

It signifies our roots and we wear it with pride, especially when abroad.

Ask any exiled ex-pats: "What reminds you of back home?"

I'm sure they would say, the Liver Bird.

I recall being in Italy on holiday, when I saw a woman wearing a t-shirt with the 'Bird' on it.

I thought she came from Liverpool.

In fact, she was an American, and she told me her father was an exiled Scouser who took great pride in his origins.

The lady was delighted that I went up to her and inquired about the 'Bird'. Incidentally, her father told her this WOULD happen.

Being an historian, I've looked at different Eagles symbolising and identifying other nations.

Two that stand out for me are the 'American Bald Eagle' and Rome's 'Sacred Roman Eagle' the Legions proudly displayed.

The powerful 'Birds' represent identity, pride, strength, courage and honour in face of adversity.

Let's not forget, Liverpool has had its fair share of adversity throughout the years. Similarly to those two global powers, we came through it all – and survived!

Yes, the 'Liver Bird' fills me with pride and honour, every time I see it or it gets mentioned.

That's what our 'Liver Bird' means to me, and always will.

" Happy Birthday!"
" Yeah..
..same to you lah!"

THE BIRD & THE ECHO

THE Liver Bird has been a part of the Liverpool ECHO masthead for decades

IT has changed in size but never in stature.

From broadsheet to tabloid, the Bird has been sitting atop of the paper - only for a brief period did it disappear, brought back by reader demand.

It is a symbol that many provincial newspaper cities would love to have instantly identifiable as the city of Liverpool.

But instead of seaweed or lyver in its beak our Liver Bird has an ECHO.

The paper even has its own life size Lily Liver Bird which appears at charity functions and promotional events.

Just as the Liver Birds have seen the city change over the past 100 years the ECHO has been there carrying the news, including a giant mechanical spider's tour of the city centre as part of 2008's Capital of Culture programme, seen far right, courtesy of Mike McCartney.

SUITES

FLY PAST FOR THE BIRDS

How Colin Lane captured a classic photograph

COLIN Lane was in the right lane when he managed to take this extraordinary photograph of the Liver Birds being treated to a fly past of honour back in 2004.

Colin, a multi award-winning photographer with Trinity Mirror, recalls the day - part of the River Festival celebrations.

"I was on my way into work and saw this plane above me circling the famous Liver Birds. They are a fantastic backdrop but this was different. I was stuck in traffic and desperate to get out and take a shot. I was, frustratingly, behind red lights, so I wound my window down, grabbed my long lens, looked up and took the pic."

The image went on to win Colin a National Photographic Award.

Colleague Martin Birchall, now a freelance photographer, praised his quick-thinking pal's work, albeit through gritted teeth...

"I was walking around all day trying to get THE picture.

"But Colin got it from his car."

The Liver Birds salute two Swordfish aeroplanes of the Royal Navy Historic Flight LS 326. This fly-past was part of the 50th anniversary of the Battle of the Atlantic in 1999. Picture by Richard Williams

A2A

That was then...

... this is now

TIMELESS

THE shots that inspire the famous Scouse wit

THE best backdrop in Liverpool for an atmospheric photograph has to be the Liver Building, Liver Birds and Clock faces. Over the years they have inspired photographers - professional and amateur - to send in images caught in unusual poses.

The ECHO enjoyed caption competitions where the wit and wisdom of Scousers came to the fore This shot, from an ECHO photographer, shows a gentle humourus reminder to readers that summer was over in 1974. The caption was: "PUT YER CLOCK BACK." Timeless!

And on the right from 1953, Mr Harold Clough of Wallasey, sent in this animated photograph.
The Statue and Liver Birds seem to be saying the same thing...

"TAXI..."

Both of them never caught one. They never will.

WHAT DO THE BIRDS DO?

BIRD SONG
By Peter Grant

Dad, what do the Liver Birds do?

Well, they look after me and, your mum and you
They've been here for a hundred years
Seen it all the - laughter and tears
They haven't aged a day
They are a real Liverpool family
You see...

Dad, but do they ever talk?
Fly off... or come down for a waterfront walk?

No, love, they are true Liverpudlians – soft, but hard
They work all day and night keeping guard
One across the sea
The other looking out to our beautiful city

Dad. what happens if they ever go away?
Or retire now they've had their 100th birthday?

No chance, love, they are here for another century
They are the spirit of Liverpool,
Here to protect and defend us all for eternity.

Dad... dad, they must get lonely up all those stairs
Can't we climb up and give them some jam
and bread
surprise them wth a bowl of Scouse... unawares

Oh no, they hear every word we've just said
C'mon let them sleep it's time for your bed.
You asked me, love, what do the Liver Birds do?
Well, look up and wave
They are always a part of me, your mum and... you

DREAM SEQUENCE

Red and Blue sky at night – Sailors' delight
Red sky in the morning – Wirral's on fire...
Dedicated to the late, great Scouse poet, Liver Bird lover and world famous author Brian Jacques.

BEAKING FROM THE HEART

NO matter where you are in the world, the Liver Birds are a symbol of home. Merseyside stars open their hearts on what these two iconic friends mean to them...

CHRISSY ROCK, ACTRESS

"To me they are Liverpool's Statue of Liberty just as the lady in New York is an emblem of that great city - our two birds are known the world over. They shout out WE ARE LIVERPOOL!"

JOHN MCARDLE, ACTOR
"I HAVE always believed and always will believe that they are the best couple of birds I have ever seen in Liverpool. Hard to chat up though."

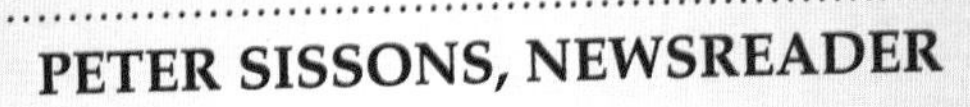

PETER SISSONS, NEWSREADER

"THE Liver Birds are the most distinctive and recognisable civil emblems in the UK, and I always get a kick out of looking up and seeing them. Other cities have moth-eaten lions, unicorns or eagles, but our big birds are unique – just like the city over which they stand guard.

And although they're house-trained, those claws and those imperious beaks say to the world "Don't mess with us!"

KIM CATTRALL, ACTRESS

"SOME lovely lady in Liverpool came up to me when I was at the Playhouse and said 'you are a real Liver Bird, luv'. I was honoured."

KEN DODD, COMEDIAN

"I TRAVEL the country playing theatres all over the UK, and the Liver Birds, to me, symbolise one thing: going HOME. I always think of Merseyside... or Mirthyside... as I call it.

They really have been a real symbol of Liverpool for 100 years and will be for the next 100 years, by Jove!

MARGI CLARKE, ACTRESS

"I WROTE my autobiography Now You See Me on the Mersey. No, I don't walk on water, but I was helped to write by my Mersey waterfront.

I sat on a boat with the reassuring River Mersey beneath me. It had to be written that way. I was within touching distance of the Liver Birds one looking out to sea and looking over me and everyone close to me the other saying "it's gonna be alright, girl."

I couldn't have - wouldn't have - written it anywhere else in the world. Thanks, you two Liver Birds, for always being YOU..."

"AS an actress it's difficult for me to have a tattoo but there is only one thing I would have tattooed - and that is the Liver Bird logo. It means a lot to me and I'd be proud to have it somewhere about my person."

"I HAVE got Liver Birds on the cover of my two books. It's just instinctive.

The Birds are naturally associated with Liverpool FC yet Everton were the first club to use the image.

If you sail into Liverpool the first thing that strikes you on seeing the waterfront are the Birds. If you are a born and bred Scouser you know you are home at last.

If you're coming here for the first time they are recognisable straight away - no other city has anything like them."

ALEX FLETCHER, ACTRESS
"I SEE them as symbol of reaching home and being home. I recall running a half marathon and seeing them in the distance as I was running through town. The nearer they got the more comforted I was that I was going to finish it."

AND THESE BIRDS CAN SING

LIVER BIRDS and music go hand in... wing

IN the early 60s there was a vibrant all female band called the Liver Birds who enjoyed succss notably in Hamburg's Star Club wheer many Liverpool male bans served their musical apprenticeships.

The group had many followers and were praised for taking on the boys in the Merseybeat surge at the time.

In 1969 The Liver Birds theme song for the TV series became a hit for the Scaffold featuring John Gorman, Mike McCartney and Roger McGough.

The lyrics capture innocence and fun.

There is the immortal line: "Yer Dancing? Yer asking?" heard in many a club, dance hall and disco.

Pop star Sonia wanted to call her album Liver Bird but record company bosses grounded that high flying idea.

In 1992 Paul McCartney the one time Wings Commander flew into Liverpool for a sell out concert at King's Dock on the banks of the Mersey with his band.

And in a throw back to The Beatles wearing smart suits the self-styled scruff from Speke made his group - including wife Linda - wear natty cream jackets sporting the Liver Bird logo.

He was home...

ALL THAT THE LIVER BIRDS HAVE SEEN

SCOTTIE ROAD

The bricks and mortar of Scottie Road may be a memory but the spirit lingers on. Featuring great photographs from the Scottie Press collection and rarely seen historical images from the League of Welldoers' Lee Jones Collection

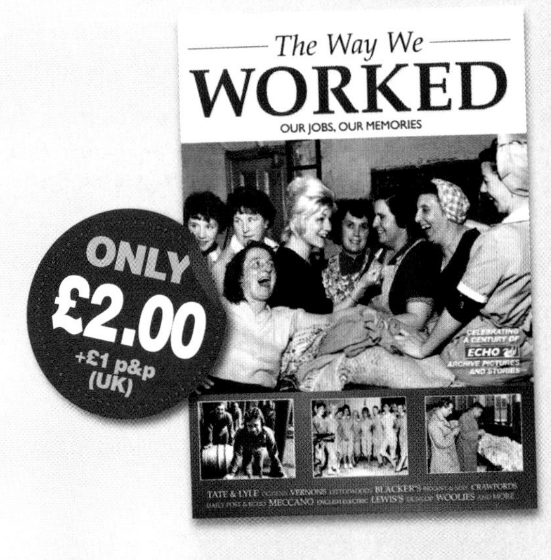

THE WAY WE WORKED

Unilever, Vernons, Littlewoods, Crawford's, Tate & Lyle, Woolies. Our jobs – our memories

NEW BRIGHTON OUR DAYS OUT REMEMBERED

Recall magical childhood summers of the golden era of what was the greatest seaside resort in the whole world

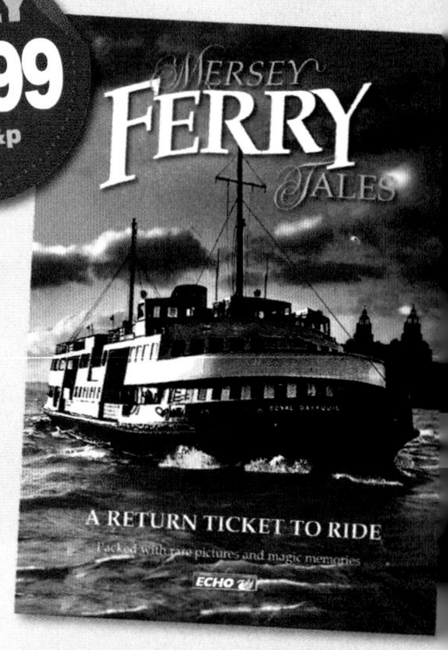

MERSEY FERRY TALES

A ticket to ride on the world's most famous ferry – a unique collection of magic maritime memories

LOST CINEMAS OF LIVERPOOL

Book your ticket for a trip down movie memory lane, to a time when Liverpool was a Tinsel Town in its own right and there was a cinema on every corner

THE LOST TRIB OF EVERTON & SCOTTIE ROAD

This nostalgic book by Ken Rogers will take you back 'home' into the inner city stre and make you feel proud

THE LOST TRIBE OF EVERTON & SCOTTIE ROAD

Ken Rogers

THE JOURNEY BACK HOME

ONLY £9.99 FREE p&p (UK)

To order call: 0845 143 0001 or visit MERSEYSHOP.COM

*** Offers while stocks last. Prices subject to change. Please telephone for international shipping rates.**

BATTLE OF BRITAIN

Packed with rare and unseen images commemorating the 70th anniversary of the Nazis' failed invasion of our shores

ONLY £2.50 FREE p&p (UK)

DUMMY BULLETS

A hilarious, thoughtful and historic story of making entertainment the secret weapon of war

ONLY £3.50 +£1 p&p (UK)

IT'S WAR

A tribute to the men, women and children who found themselves thrust into the deadliest conflict in human history

ONLY £1.00 +£1 p&p (UK)

MERSEY BLITZ

This special publication marks the 70th anniversary of the May blitz, when the Luftwaffe rained bombs, land mines and incendiary devices on Liverpool

ONLY £3.99 +£1 p&p (UK)

LIVER COOL

AUTHENTIC souvenirs of the most famous Birds in the world...

Off the Cuff

Only £64.80 +£4.25 p&p (UK)

Passport Cover

Silver Bird
Pewter Bird
Keepsake

Only £84.00 +£5.99 p&p (UK)

Handy! Liver Bird Bracelet

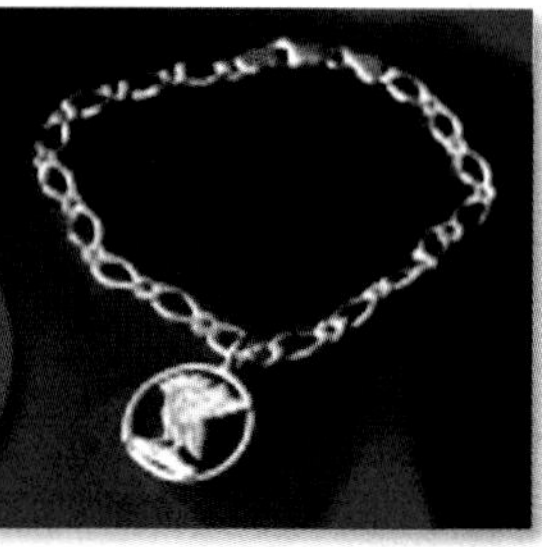

Necklace Pendant

Only £54.20 +£4.25 p&p (UK)

To order call: 0845 143 0001 or visit
MERSEYSHOP.COM

1911 – the Liver Birds were born (if you look at the clock you can see the timing's just right). Photographer Tony Hall's magical illustration (there were no mobile phone cameras back then) captures a new dawn – and a new era. The most unique legendary twins in the world

UPWARDS AND ONWARDS

Here's to you, Liver Birds

SO, dear fine feathered friends, it's time to move on. One hundred years not out and you are going from strength to strength. So much has happened from 1911 to the present day.

You are two skyline stars who have stayed loyal to the city. Copper wire holds you both down, you could have broken away and flown off, but you stayed put.

So, as we toast you being here for the last century, Let's crack open the champagne and toast to the next one.

There will be more changes in Liverpool; there will more sadness and yet more triumphs. Keep on watchng over us - you are well-loved at home and abroad.

Liver Birds live on... forever.

"I AM A LIVER BIRD"
– KIM CATTRALL

They are iconic . . . they are a very real couple, who have spent their lives with their backs to each other. They don't talk, but they speak volumes. No, it's not Lennon and McCartney. Born in 1911, they are celebrating 100 years perched high over Liverpool looking into the city and out across the Mersey.
They have seen everything from the First and Second World Wars, the 50s, 60s 70s, 80s and 90s. Then they smiled again when Liverpool became European Capital of Culture in 2008.
Like a Phoenix, the Liver Bird rises and rises again.
If they ever take off and fly away Liverpool is no more. No chance of that, la, as Scousers say. They have seen and heard it all and now, through our new stunning 84-page publication, a Bird's Eye View, packed with Liverpool Daily Post and Echo archive photographs and stories from celebrities who all fell in love with these two world famous characters.
New York has The Statue of Liberty, France has the Eiffel Tower . . . Liverpool has The Liver Birds – this is a celebration for generations to keep and treasure.
They have flown all over the world – but never once left Liverpool . . .
Happy 100th birthday, Liver Birds.

£3.99

ISBN 978-1-906802-83-7

ALTON DOUGLAS PRESENTS

THE BIRMINGHAM SCRAPBOOK VOL I